Flowers

Written by Emily Bone

Illustrated by Samara Hardy

Designed by Zoe Wray

Reading consultant:
Alison Kelly

Some flowers are big and open.
This is a sunflower.

Some flowers are closed and tight.

Tulips

Other
flowers
are small.

Blanket
flower

Different flowers have different kinds of leaves.

Wiggly

Spiky

Round

Thin

Shiny

Furry

Flowers grow from seeds.
A root grows down.

Seed

Root

A shoot grows up above the
ground. Small leaves grow
from the shoot.

Shoot

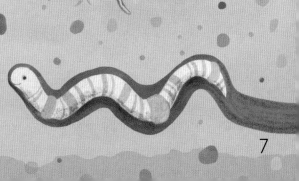

At first, a flower is small.
Its leaves grow bigger.
Stems grow. Then buds grow.

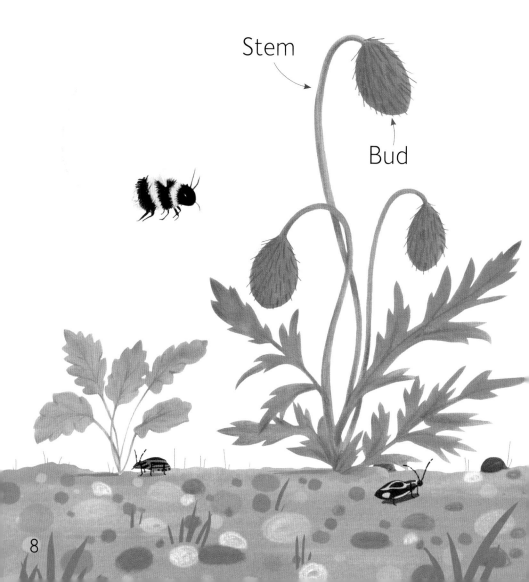

Stem

Bud

When the
buds open
flowers appear.

9

Flowers make a sweet
liquid called nectar.

Bees drink
nectar.

Bees fly from flower to flower,
drinking the nectar from
different ones.

Other animals drink nectar
from flowers, too.

Hummingbird

Beetle

Butterfly

Bats and moths
drink nectar
at night.

Fruit grows from flowers.

The petals fall off.
A green strawberry grows.

The strawberry
turns red.

Birds sometimes
eat the fruit.

In the spring, trees grow flowers.

Horse chestnut trees
have tall flowers.

Cherry tree flowers
are small and pink.

Magnolia trees
have flowers with
big, open petals.

Catkin flowers are long and thin.
They look different from other flowers.

They dangle
from branches.

Catkins grow on birch trees.

This is a dandelion. It grows a bright yellow flower.

The petals fall off.
Then fluffy seeds grow.

The wind blows
and the seeds
float away.

In a desert, it doesn't rain very often.

Cactus plants grow
in the desert.

Desert plants grow lots of flowers
when it does rain. Flowers grow
on the ground, too.

Plants grow in ponds and rivers.
Their roots are under the water.

Some plants
have flowers and
leaves that sit
on the surface.

Plants grow flowers
on tall stems above
the water, too.

Lots of different flowers
grow in a rainforest.

Most flowers grow
high up so they get
lots of sunlight.

Some grow on
the trunks and
branches of trees.

The biggest flower in the
world is a rafflesia.

It grows on the ground in
the rainforest.

It can grow as big
as the wheel on
a truck.

A flower starts to die. Its petals droop and fall off.

It grows a pod
full of seeds.

The wind blows the
pod from side to
side. Seeds fall
to the ground.

Each seed grows
into a new plant.

Digital retouching by John Russell

First published in 2015 by Usborne Publishing Ltd., Usborne House, 83-85 Saffron Hill, London
EC1N 8RT England. www.usborne.com Copyright © 2015 Usborne Publishing Ltd. The name
Usborne and the devices ♀♔ are Trade Marks of Usborne Publishing Ltd. All rights reserved.
No part of this publication may be reproduced, stored in a retrieval system, or transmitted in
any form or by any means, electronic, mechanical, photocopying, recording or otherwise
without the prior permission of the publisher. First published in America 2016. U.E.